Museum of Antiquities

Stories from the Northern Frontier

Created by

Jo Catling and Arlene Rankin

with children from

Stobhillgate First School, Morpeth
St. Michael's Church of England First School, Alnwick

and

Barbara Hutchinson

Published by
The Museum of Antiquities of the University and Society of Antiquaries of Newcastle upon Tyne
Newcastle University
Newcastle upon Tyne
NE1 7RU

Copyright © Creators and Newcastle University 2007. All rights reserved.
No part of this book may be reproduced, stored in a retrieval system, or transmitted, in any form or by any means, electronic,
mechanical, photocopying, recording or otherwise, without the prior written permission of the Publisher.

ISBN 978-0-7017-0214-4

Contents

There was once a Roman God called Hercules. He was Jupiter's champion, strong and brave.

He was so strong that when he was a baby he wrestled two serpents sent to murder him by Juno, Jupiter's jealous wife, and killed them.

One day Eurystheus, Juno's champion, gave Hercules an extra challenging task. He commanded Hercules to find the golden apples that grew on the Tree of Life.

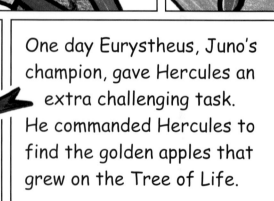

The garden where the tree grew was a beautiful sight. Tall golden flowers, snow white daisies and soft green grass swayed in the warm breeze.

Four lovely ladies looked after the tree but they were so bored that they ate all the apples!

7

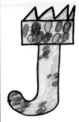uno, queen of the gods, found out about this and put a serpent in the garden to watch over the ladies.

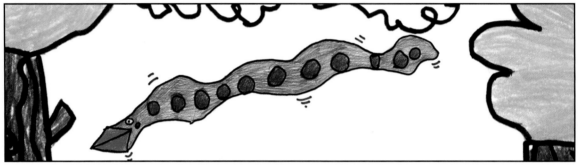

Hercules set off on his quest. He searched for the sea god Nereus who knew where the golden apples grew. As he was travelling through Illyria he met some water nymphs who told him where to find Nereus.

When he found him Hercules grabbed Nereus and squeezed him so tightly that his face went purple and he couldn't breathe. He was forced to tell him where the lovely ladies were.

POPPED

On Hercules went to Libya. When he got there the king, Anateus, forced Hercules to wrestle! Hercules had heard that the king couldn't be beaten if his feet touched the ground. So he charged Anateus, head-butting him in the stomach and winding him. Then Hercules wrapped his arms around his waist and with an enormous heave lifted him off the ground, squishing him so that his bones popped!

Hercules was very tired but knew he had to carry on. He left Libya and crossed into Egypt. It was the custom here to sacrifice strangers to Jupiter to stop famines.

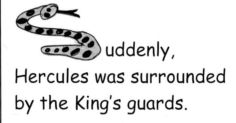

Suddenly, Hercules was surrounded by the King's guards.

He was dragged and tied to an altar. Hercules was so powerful that he just burst the ropes and killed the King and his son.

At last Hercules came to the mountains where the garden grew. Here Atlas, a giant, held up the sky. Hercules offered to hold the sky for awhile if Atlas would get the apples.

Atlas agreed but when he returned he refused to take the sky back. "I'll take the apples to King Eurystheus," he said.

"Okay," said Hercules, "but I need a pillow for my head." Atlas took back the mountain. Hercules grabbed the apples and ran off laughing.

Finally, Hercules could return home. Atlas was left holding the sky. After a long time he changed into a mountain himself... and he's still there!

Dylan

Rachel

Abbie

Aithne

Daniel

Lexy

WRITTEN AND ILLUSTRATED BY

THE CHILDREN OF

ST MICHAEL'S CHURCH OF ENGLAND FIRST SCHOOL

ALNWICK

Georgice

Shania

michael

mark

Long, long ago there were two kings
called Numitor and Amulius.
They ruled over a country called Alba Longa.
Amulius looked after all the money
and Numitor made the laws.

Amulius was greedy.
He wanted to be the
only king so he fought
Numitor and beat
him up...

Go away now.

and **never** return.

...and sent him into
away from his

exile...

family.

Numitor's daughter, Rhea Silvia, was sent away to become a Vestal Virgin. Vestal Virgins were not supposed to get married or have babies.

One day the god Mars saw Rhea Silvia. He fell madly in love with her.

Some time later she gave birth to handsome twin boys.

Amulius was FURIOUS!
He ordered one of his slaves to kill the twins but the slave couldn't do it. He thought it was too cruel so he put them into a basket and left it by the River Tiber.

The river flooded and the basket floated away.

Tiberius, the god of the river, kept them safe.

The basket got caught in the roots of a fig tree where they were found by a she-wolf who took care of them.

One day a shepherd called Faustulus saw the wolf with the twins and took them home to his wife.

They named the boys Romulus and Remus.

The boys grew up to be tall, brave and very handsome. They worked with Faustulus and the other shepherds. But one day…

Hey, get off my sheep.

Ha! Ha! Come on, try and stop us.

Say goodbye to your sheep!

…Numitor's shepherds stole sheep from Romulus and Remus. There was a fight and the shepherds were hurt.

Remus was arrested and taken to Numitor but Romulus wasn't caught because he was busy praying to the gods.

My grandsons!

Numitor was impressed by Remus' strength and intelligence. He wondered who he was. Remus told him how he and his brother had been found on a river bank by a she-wolf. As he listened Numitor realised that the twins were his grandsons!

He sent for Romulus and told both boys what had happened to him and their mother.

Romulus and Remus were furious. They went and found their Great Uncle Amulius and killed him.

Romulus and Remus went back to live with their grandfather who was now king of Alba Longa.

A few years later they decided to build their own city on one of the hills near the River Tiber. The twins argued about where to build it. Romulus chose the Palatine Hill but Remus thought that the Capitoline Hill was a better site.

I want it here.

No, I want it here.

They both made sacrifices to Mars, and asked him to make the choice for them. Mars chose the Palatine Hill.

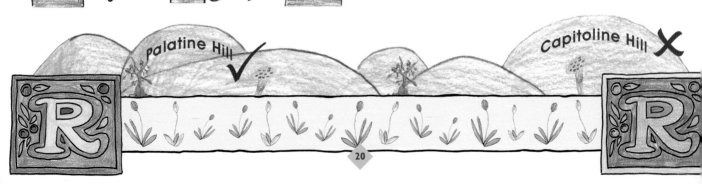

Palatine Hill ✓

Capitoline Hill ✗

Ha! Ha! I jumped over your wall.

Remus and Romulus still argued. Remus teased Romulus about the height of his walls, saying they were much too low. To prove it he jumped over them and laughed loudly.

Romulus was really angry so he fought his brother and killed him!

Grrr... I need to make my walls higher.

Romulus became king of the new city. It was called Rome.

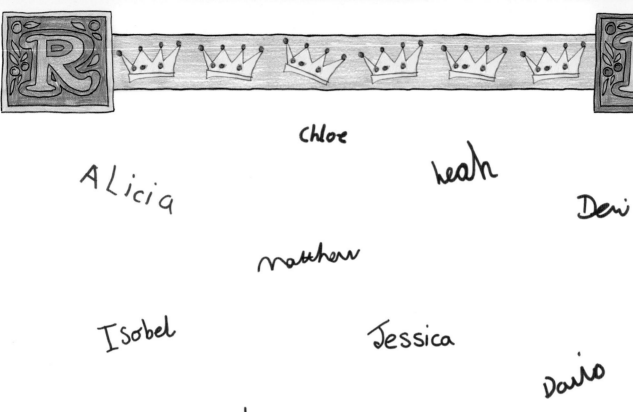

Chloe

Leah

Alicia

Deni

Matthew

Isobel

Jessica

Dailo

Lacey

Ross

Shea

Written and illustrated by
the children of
St Michael's Church of England First School
Alnwick

AND HIS AMAZING ELEPHANTS

A LONG TIME AGO, IN A NORTH AFRICAN CITY CALLED CARTHAGE THERE LIVED A MAN CALLED HANNIBAL.

CARTHAGE

THAT'S ME!

The people of Carthage had ruled over a huge empire but after many battles they had lost all their land to the Romans. Hannibal's dad, Hamilcar, was determined to build an even better empire. He took his army and fought the people of Hispania. Young Hannibal went with him.

FANTASTIC - WE'RE THE GREATEST.

YEEES! WE'VE WON AGAIN LADS.

When he was nine Hannibal made a solemn promise...

HANNIBAL, THE ROMANS MUST BE YOUR LIFELONG ENEMIES.

I SWEAR DAD!

...and eventually he took command of the army.

I'M AUDAX ELEPHANTUS. LOOK OUT FOR ME ON EVERY PAGE OF THIS STORY!

HANNIBAL HAD A PROBLEM...

...how was he going to get his elephants across the wide river?

He got his soldiers to build huge, wooden rafts. Very carefully he led the elephants onto them. The rafts were very slippery!

Hannibal and his army happily marched alongside one of the rivers leading from the magnificent River Rhône. By Autumn they had arrived at the foot of the Alps.

When Hannibal arrived at the Alps he faced an even greater challenge; his army had to climb up the mountains!

YEEES! WE'VE MADE IT AT LAST!!!

Hannibal didn't give up. He marched all his men and the elephants over the Alps. They were all very cold and tired. The mountain tribes attacked them! But eventually they got across the Alps.

GET OUT OF OUR WAY.

YOU'RE NOT GETTING PAST US!

OH YES WE WILL!

YOU'LL ALL DIE!

IT'S NOT HALF COLD.

HANNIBAL LED HIS ARMY DOWN THE MOUNTAINS TO THE FLAT PLAINS OF ITALIA.

Italy

I DON'T BELIEVE IT!

HOW DID THEY DO THAT?

AAAGH!

The Romans could not believe their ears when they heard that Hannibal had crossed the Alps.

OH MY POOR, BRAVE ELEPHANTS.

Even though Hannibal arrived with only half of his soldiers and lots of the elephants died, he went on to win three great battles against the Romans.

It was another sixteen years before Hannibal was finally defeated, but no-one since has tried to march elephants over the Alps!

Bethany ♥

Caitlin

Hannah-marie
x x

Edris

Jordan

Sasha

Emm-Louise

Poppy ♥

WRITTEN AND ILLUSTRATED BY
THE CHILDREN OF
ST MICHAEL'S CHURCH OF ENGLAND FIRST SCHOOL
ALNWICK

Welcome, Julius Caesar, this is your life! Born in a shabby house in a run down part of Roma no-one could have known how famous your name would become.

WHO'S WHO IN ROMA !

Patrician - most important people in Roma; usually very rich. Caesar's family were patricians.

You were a keen pupil and worked hard for your teachers, studying alongside your two sisters. Life wasn't all work though; you enjoyed wrestling and playing knucklebones with your friends.

83BC

Bending to tie his shoes one morning your father had a heart attack and died; you were sixteen. Now you are head of the household. A year later you became High Priest at Jupiter's temple.

The family celebrations continued when you married Cornelia and hopes for a brighter future were high.

Sadly, those bright hopes came to nothing. Enemies plotted against you and your fortunes changed. You lost your job at the temple and had to leave Roma in a hurry.

But you're not one to give up, are you? You join the Roman army and become a very clever general. Fearlessly you lead your men into many battles, winning honour for the people of Roma.

You still find time to study and this leads you into trouble. While travelling to meet a great teacher you're captured by pirates who imprison you. They demand 50 talents of gold for your release. You vow to take revenge!

As soon as you are released, you gather your own fleet of ships and capture the pirates. All of them are executed as a warning to others!

69 BC

WHO'S WHO IN ROMA 2
Aedile - looks after buildings and markets. Puts on games, gladiator fights etc.

Back in Roma, you are given a new job as an aedile. You organize spectacular horse races and gladiator fights that keep the crowds entertained.

WHO'S WHO IN ROMA 3
Consul - head of Roman government; the most powerful person in the Empire.

You order the construction of lots of wonderful buildings which makes you very popular with the people. In 60 BC you achieve your highest honour when you are elected Consul of Roma!

There is no limit to your talents. You are made governor of Gallia and lead the army in many battles against the fearsome Gallic tribes. Finally you defeat them at the battle of Alesia and capture their leader Vercingetorix.

Not content with victory over the Gauls you try twice to invade Britannia but both times your ships are destroyed by storms and you have to give up. You must have found this very hard to do.

Caesar, break up your army and come back to Roma.

NO! I won't.

WHO'S WHO IN ROMA 4

Senators - rich men who rule Roma. Together they are the Senate.

You are so successful that some senators worry that you might demand to be made king. They order you to break up your army and return home. You refuse and cross the River Rubicon, marching straight into Roma to meet them!

ROME

DID YOU KNOW?

The River Rubicon flows between Gallia and Italia.

Rubicon River

Roma

By now you are the most powerful man in the Roman Republic. The senators are determined to stop you and send an army to capture you. Battles take place around the Mediterranean Sea but you defeat all your enemies.

While you are fighting in Egypt you meet the beautiful Queen Cleopatra. You fall deeply in love with her and have a son together, but sadly your love won't last long.

We move on to the Ides of February earlier this year. Special games were held to celebrate your great victories. Your dear friend Mark Anthony asked you to become king, but you refused.

Your enemies see that you have become a dictator and plot against you behind your back. They even manage to persuade your best friend, Brutus, to join them.

At last we come to the events of today, the Ides of March. The senators ask you to meet them. As you make your way across the city a fortune teller warns you not to go but you ignore her, a very foolish mistake.

Ethan   Connor   IMOGEN

craig   chloe

                                              Scott

HAYLEY   ♡   Andrew
                     ★
                    Ruby

        Zach   Michael

                  DEMI

Lenny   Vic

    Corrine   Daniel

Katie

WRITTEN and ILLUSTRATED BY THE CHILDREN OF
ST MICHAEL'S CHURCH of ENGLAND FIRST SCHOOL, ALNWICK

One day, when the World was young, the Sun floated gently in the light blue sky.

The Sun was sad that the World was empty. No birds sang and no flowers bloomed.

The Sun knew that the Primeval Bull had the power to bring all the animals and plants to the world.

He needed Mithras to kill the Bull so that the World could have life.

46

Mithras thought this was a terrible idea and he refused to do it.

Mithras reluctantly changed his mind and agreed to help.

Oh **alright!** I'll help kill the Primeval Bull.

He went into the meadow with Cautes and Cautopates...

...and they tried to capture the Bull.

The Bull was determined not to be caught and charged at the three friends.

Cautes and Cautopates threw a net over the Bull and captured it.

Mithras managed to drag the Bull by its back
legs into a big, dark cave.

Inside the cave Mithras pushed, pulled, tugged and wrestled with the Bull.

Eventually he managed to throw the Bull onto the floor. He stamped his foot on its back.

He pulled out his dagger and...

..killed it!

A few minutes passed before Mithras and his two exhausted helpers dragged the Bull to the Moon Goddess.

She cleansed the Bull's body and suddenly all the animals tumbled out.

Each creature eventually found its own place in the world.

The Sun was...

DELIGHTED!

Mithras had brought life to Earth!

Bethy

KANe

Rebecca

Alex

Nyle

Rohan

WRITTEN AND ILLUSTRATED

BY

THE CHILDREN OF

ST MICHAEL'S CHURCH OF ENGLAND FIRST SCHOOL

ALNWICK

Aimee

Paul

Rebecca

michael

My name is Maia.

My Dad Festus trains war elephants for Emperor Claudius.

This is my favourite elephant, Magnus.

This is the story of how my Dad and I travelled with Emperor Claudius when he invaded Britannia.

This is how it all started.

Emperor Claudius had a message from Verica, a friendly prince from one of the British tribes.

He was being attacked by enemy tribes. He needed some help.

Emperor Claudius commanded his officer Aulus Plautius to go to Britannia and help Verica.

He took with him a huge army of four legions - 40,000 men altogether!

Plautius and his men marched towards the River Tamesis. They fought lots of battles. At last they came to the riverbank.

There was a fierce, crowded battle and blood flooded everywhere.

Togodumnus, the king of the Catuvellauni tribe, was killed. The rest of the tribes were sad at his death.

They swore to take revenge.

Plautius ordered his men to build a camp.

He sent a letter to Emperor Claudius to come and fight with him in the last battle.

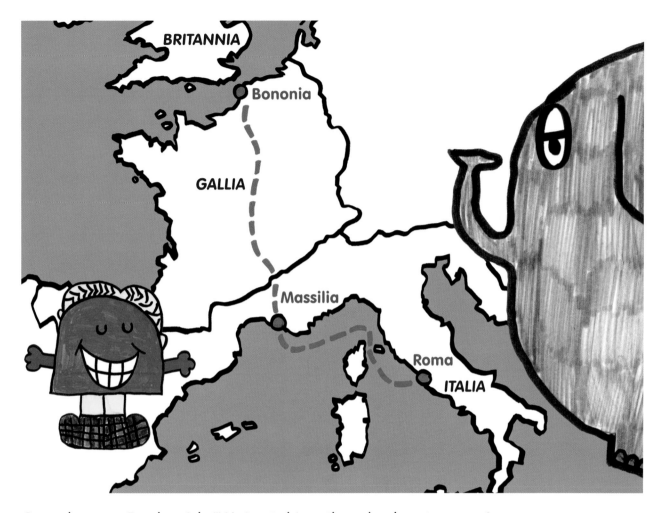

One day my Dad said, "We're taking the elephants on a journey. Pack your things and get Magnus ready."

We set out from Roma and sailed down the River Tiber until we reached Ostia. From there we all went to Massilia where we stopped for something to eat and drink.

After a short stop in Massilia, Magnus and I travelled through Gallia with the Emperor and everyone else.

We passed rushing rivers and dark forests. It was amazing! I had never seen this country before. There were singing birds everywhere.

We were nearly at Bononia when I saw something out of the corner of my eye, it was a pig!

I was worried about Magnus because I knew he was terrified of pigs.

"Run," I squealed.

Magnus ran, we all held onto him and dashed away.

The pig was out of sight. We slowed down.

At last we reached Bononia.

We had to persuade the elephants to get on the ships then we sailed to Britannia. It was a long journey.

I remembered the stories I'd heard about the legions...

The soldiers wouldn't board the ships because they were petrified. They thought ghosts and evil spirits lived in Britannia.

Plautius sent a message to Claudius asking for help.

Claudius sent Narcissus, his special advisor, to persuade the men to get on the ships. The men were embarrassed, after all they were soldiers! One brave man marched up the gangplank and the rest quickly followed.

There was a very big storm, the ships slipped from side to side, the soldiers were frightened.

Then they saw a shooting star moving from the east across to the west, the direction they were sailing in.

This was a good sign!

At last we landed in Britannia.

We all marched to the River Tamesis to meet up with Plautius and the Legions.

Emperor Claudius led the Legions against the British tribes. The British were brave but they were still defeated!

Our elephants charged the last warriors and frightened them from the battlefield.

We marched with the army on to Camulodunum, the capital of the Catuvellauni!

There was a parade. Emperor Claudius was at the front. Magnus was next and I rode on his back. The British children stared at us.

And that was the end of my adventure.

Except to say, look at the flag. What do you think? Can you believe it?

Magnus is carrying a wild pig!!

Megan

Chelsea

R.Pringle

THE END

Zoe

Written and illustrated by
the children of
Stobhillgate First School
Morpeth

Sofina

Brandon

Anna

We acknowledge the inspiration of Roger Hargreaves and the Mr Men

CARATACUS
And
CARTIMANDUA

The Britons Fight Back

Introduction

The Romans invaded Britannia in AD 43. They arrived in huge wooden boats.

Caratacus was leader of the Catuvellauni tribe that lived in the south of Britannia and he wasn't happy.

Cartimandua was Queen of the Brigantes tribe. She lived in the north of Britannia and she was worried.

These are their stories.

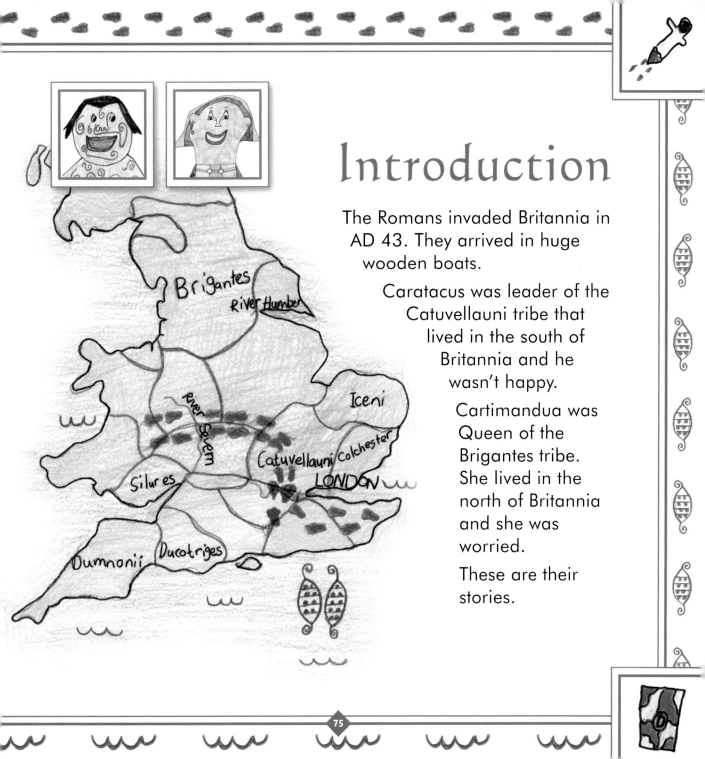

Brigantes

River Humber

Iceni

River Severn

Catuvellauni Colchester

LONDON

Silures

Dumnonii

Ducotriges

The Romans defeated Caratacus at the Battle of the River Thames. At the end of the day he looked across the battlefield. Many Britons lay dead and dying, among them his brother Togodumnus. He had been a brave man but there was nothing Caratacus could do. Sadly he and his army retreated.

Caratacus continued to fight against the invaders, sometimes he was successful and sometimes his men just managed to escape with their lives. Leaders of other tribes came with their warriors to join him. Together they hoped to defeat the Romans once and for all.

Cartimandua's story

Cartimandua was a powerful queen. Her lands stretched from the east of Britannia almost to the west coast. She lived in a roundhouse with her husband Venutius. Venutius was a very lazy man, which annoyed Cartimandua because she had always been lively. Even as a young girl she enjoyed hunting with her father, the king.

This is the inside of a roundhouse with meat hanging from the roof of the house.

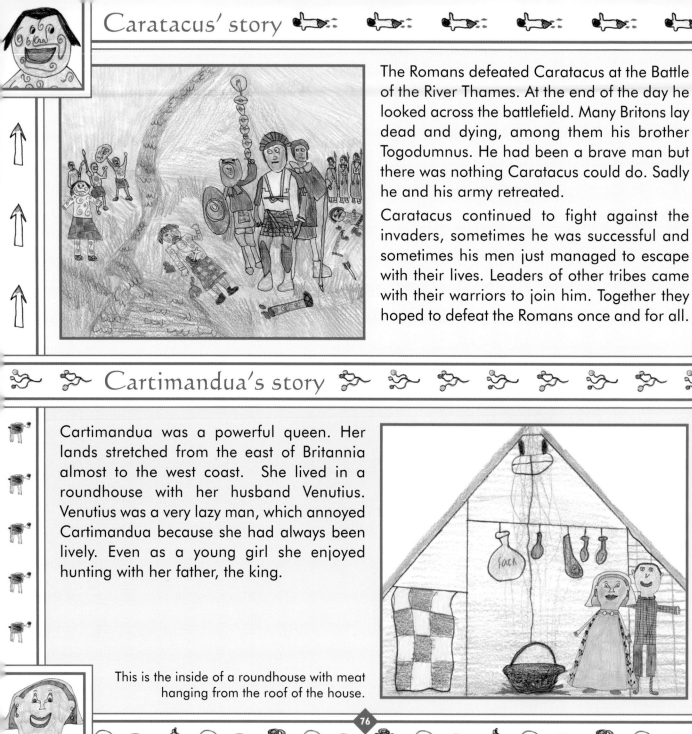

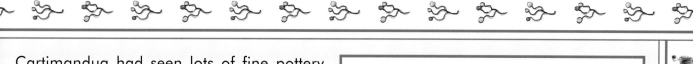

Years went by and the Romans grew more frustrated with Caratacus. By AD 51 he and his men were holding out against the Roman army in a hillfort on the banks of the River Severn.

Ostorius Scapula, the Roman commander, wanted to defeat the Britons once and for all. He led his army across the river and marched towards the fort. They must have been a frightening sight. Before the battle Caratacus gave a great speech to encourage his warriors. They all cheered and promised to fight to the death!

Cartimandua had seen lots of fine pottery and glass from Rome and she knew about the Romans and their victories against the Southern tribes. Venutius hated the Romans and wanted to fight them, but she wasn't sure this was a good idea. She was worried that they might take over.

Maybe the gods would show her a way to stop them.

Scapula shouted orders to his centurions and the soldiers attacked Caratacus' hillfort with all their courage and strength. The British warriors threw spears and rocks down at the Romans but it was no good and eventually the soldiers broke through the wooden gates. The hillfort was in ruins. There was killing and death everywhere. Caratacus knew the battle was lost! He ordered his people to try and escape, but for some it was too late.

For a long while life for the Brigantes carried on as normal. Sometimes travellers brought news of the latest Roman victory but usually the talk around the village fires was of hunting and harvests.

Caratacus' wife and daughter were among the captured Britons. They were really horrified because they didn't know what the Romans were going to do with them. They thought that they might be killed! Luckily they were just kept prisoners. They wondered what had happened to Caratacus. He might be starving, or worse, he might be dead!

Meanwhile, Caratacus was travelling north to the Brigantes with his remaining warriors, he didn't realise that their queen was already friendly with the Romans!

One day Druid messengers arrived with a message for Queen Cartimandua from Caratacus. Would she and her tribe join him in the fight against the Romans? The gods had sent their answer.

She sent a messenger to Scapula. When he reached him he said, "Caratacus is coming to Queen Cartimandua's fort. She will make him really drowsy by giving him lots and lots of beer and wine and then you can get him!"

 The betrayal was prepared!

Cartimandua welcomed Caratacus and his men to her village, where she had prepared a great feast in his honour. Everyone was invited and there was much eating and drinking. The musicians played late into the night.

After the feast Caratacus fell into a deep sleep, just as Cartimandua had planned!

In the early morning Roman soldiers crept up towards Cartimandua's fort. They were let in by the sneaky Brigantes. The Romans surrounded Caratacus while he still slept in a pile of hay. Five legionaries jumped on top of him and held him down while two soldiers pulled a dusty flour sack over Caratacus' head. He immediately started coughing from the dust and began to struggle and fight his captors. It was no use, there were just too many of them. Caratacus was dragged like a slave to the Roman headquarters, where he was beaten and battered.

Caratacus was locked in chains and taken as a prisoner to Italia. His name was well known across the Roman Empire. People admired him for his bravery, cunning and honour. He would be the most prized captive in the Emperor's Triumph through the streets of Roma.

TRIUMPH
A parade through the streets of Rome held in honour of an emperor who had won a great victory.

Meanwhile back at the roundhouse...

Scapula was very pleased to have Caratacus as a prisoner.

Cartimandua and her husband were given beautiful pottery and fine jewellery. She started to build a grand house.

Venutius enjoyed his new life style; eating, drinking and lounging about. "Get me more wine!" he ordered the slaves.

Caratacus and his family were paraded in front of the citizens of Roma. At the end of the procession the prisoners expected to be killed. All of them were were very afraid except Caratacus who looked proudly in front of him. When he was taken to Emperor Claudius, Caratacus spoke bravely about his right to be free and not a slave to the Romans. He told Claudius, "If you save my life I shall remind people of your mercy forever."

Cartimandua got fed up. She wanted a new man. Vellocatus, her husband's servant, was brave, young and good looking, unlike the lazy, fat Venutius. "I'm fed up of you," she screamed to Venutius, "I'm divorcing you!" She married Vellocatus.

The Emperor liked what the Briton said and gave him his freedom. He was re-united with his family and for many years they lived in Rome where they were treated with honour by the people.

The tribe was furious with Cartimandua. "Our queen has married someone half her age," they muttered. "What is she doing?" Venutius and the men gathered together to attack her. Cartimandua and her new husband feared for their lives. She sent lots of messages to her Roman friends to come and protect her. The Roman army came. Cartimandua and Vellocatus fled the village and spent the rest of their lives in exile.

Venutius ruled the tribe. He carried on fighting the Romans and after lots of battles he was defeated in AD 71. The Brigantes people became part of the Roman Empire like the other British tribes.

Eventually they got used to Roman rule. New roads brought traders to their villages, the children learnt to speak Latin and some even joined the Roman Army.

The Empire was here to stay and for the next 300 years Britannia would be governed from Rome.

Georgia

Lucas

Hollie

Daniel

Sadia

Matthew. J

Nathalie

CARATACUS
And
CARTIMANDUA

Written and illustrated by
the children of
Stobhillgate First School
Morpeth

Vicky

Paul

Kieran

Bethany

Charley-louise

Sally

Jonathan

Matthew O

Ayleisha

JULIA LUCILLA

A Senator's Daughter at the Edge of the Empire

JULIA

Salvete! My name is Julia Lucilla, daughter of Senator Julius Lucillus. For many years I travelled around the Empire with my husband, Rufinus, and now I'm back in Roma, I'd like to share with you some of my letters home from my last journey.

RUFINUS

My Husband, Prefect of the Cohort of Vardulli at High Rochester

EMPEROR SEPTIMUS

The most important Roman

JULIA DOMNA

Septimus' Wife

AMELIA

My friend in Roma

EUTYCHUS

A freedman and my right-hand man

This is a map of my travels.

My Dear Amelia,

We've just arrived in Britannia.
I was very seasick on the ship
so I couldn't enjoy the galley
slaves' cooking.

I've sent you a shell
necklace that I bought in
Petuaria from one of the traders
by the quayside.

I miss you already.
May the gods keep you safe.

Your Julia

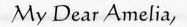

My Dear Amelia,

Today I travelled northwards with Eutychus for company, Rufinus was in front with his men. It's not at all like Italia; the roads are good but dangerous, so wherever we go soldiers have to come with us. The wild flowers are beautiful but there are no vineyards, just small fields of corn.

We should soon be at Eburacum. When we get there I'm going to ask the ladies which plants can be used for cooking and making medicine.

I've dried some flowers for you to look at. They're inside the writing tablet.

I look forward to receiving your letter when we reach Eburacum.

May the gods keep you safe.

Your Julia

? **Raeda:** A four-wheeled carriage pulled by horses. It travelled about 20 miles in a day.

My Dear Amelia,

It's been so exciting! When we reached Eburacum we were invited by Julia Domna to a birthday celebration in honour of Emperor Septimus.

You would have really enjoyed it. Julia Domna just talked and talked. She wanted to know all the latest gossip from Roma. We had a happy evening comparing hairstyles and dresses and moaning about the price of slaves!

We ate lots of lovely food, the honey cakes were deliciously sticky. We listened to beautiful music played on lyres and pipes.

I have sent you a brooch I bought from a local craftsman in Eburacum.

Farewell my dearest friend.

Julia

Julia Lucilla, to my friend Amelia, Greetings.

Well, after many goodbyes we've left Eburacum behind us. Rufinus made an offering to Mercury, seeking his protection for our journey.

The road to Coria and the Great Wall was busy but most of the travellers were soldiers. The Cursus Publicus raced past us - I wished we'd been going that fast!

Coria has been badly damaged in raids by fierce northern tribes, but I was pleased to see that the market was still busy as I need to stock up for Bremenium before we leave.

?

Cursus publicus: The imperial postal service. Its messengers travelled 40 miles in a day.

It seemed an age before we drew up at the inn; I was very weary and looking forward to a good soak in the baths.

Your loving friend
Julia Lucilla

My Dear Amelia,

How I hate it here.
It rains all the time with huge
thunderstorms.

The last part of our journey was
frightful. We lost the wheel on our
carriage and then a fog came down. Eutychus and I got lost and
when it cleared we found ourselves alone in the middle of a
forest. Luckily Eutychus found a track that led us back to the
road. Everyone was waiting anxiously for us. We told them
what had happened. Thank the gods we were safe because
people often get killed.

Wish you were here,
keep safe.

From Julia Lucilla

My dearest friend Amelia

After our narrow escape Eutychus asked the stone mason to make an altar to thank the god *Silvanus* for keeping us safe in the forest. He can't put it up in the garden yet because it's too big for him to do on his own. We need a strong soldier to help him!

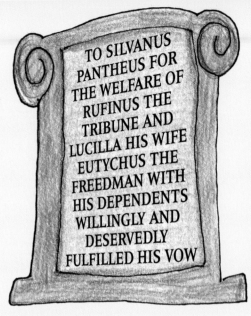

TO SILVANUS PANTHEUS FOR THE WELFARE OF RUFINUS THE TRIBUNE AND LUCILLA HIS WIFE EUTYCHUS THE FREEDMAN WITH HIS DEPENDENTS WILLINGLY AND DESERVEDLY FULFILLED HIS VOW

We are settling into our new home. Rufinus is kept busy guarding the road north against the local tribes.

Our cook makes really great food, Amelia, I wish you were here to taste it!

That's all for now.

Your loving friend

Julia Lucilla

Julia Lucilla to my friend Amelia,

How different my life is from yours in Roma. It is too dangerous for me to go outside the fort walls.

The prefect's wife at nearby Habitancum invited me to pay a visit. It isn't safe for me to travel alone and soldiers can't be spared to go with me, everyone is too busy.

I wish I could go because I'm feeling lonely. I use the fort bath house which is lovely and warm in this cold, damp climate, but it isn't the same without a friend to chat to!

My husband works very hard and I'm worried for his health, after all he's not as young as he was.

I'm glad of the plants in the herb garden. I use them to make Rufinus a refreshing, soothing tonic to drink.

Julia Lucilla

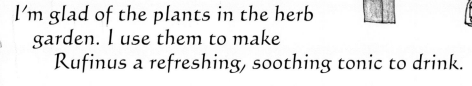

To Amelia,

I have got terrible news. My wonderful husband is dead.

Eutychus has been so good to me. He helped me plan Rufinus' funeral. We put a tombstone on his grave as well as flowers. They smelt lovely. I wanted everyone to know what a good man he was and how much I loved him.

I wish that you were here, Amelia. I have to leave and come back to Roma so I will see you soon.

I am so sad that Rufinus has died but I look forward to greeting you once again my very good friend.

Farewell

Julia Lucilla

THE END

Garry

Mark

Munina

Callum

Bethany

Written and illustrated by
the children of
Stobhillgate First School
Morpeth

Emma

Megan

Amy

A long time ago, in the wild, boggy landscape of Northumberland, there lived a beautiful goddess called Coventina.

She lived with three elegant nymphs who served her loyally.

Coventina was the goddess of a clear, sparkling spring but she was very sad.

She was meant to be worshipped like all the other gods and goddesses, but only a passing shepherd or wild animals visited her to drink the cool, refreshing water.

Then one day Roman engineers arrived. They shouted orders to the soldiers who built walls to make a fort.

When the shepherd saw the soldiers he said, "You'll need some fresh water for your fort. I can show you where there's a spring."

The engineers ordered the soldiers to build a wall around Coventina's spring to make a well. They piped the water up to the fort so that the soldiers could have clean water for drinking, washing and for their animals.

Coventina was delighted because the soldiers and their families visited her to offer gifts in return for her help.

Many years later a new religion called Christianity spread throughout the Empire. The Emperor commanded that all the temples and shrines to Roman gods be demolished.

The people carefully took down Coventina's altars and incense burners and placed them gently in the well.

In her fury Coventina FLOODED the land!

In time the Roman army marched away to fight in Rome and it was never seen again.

Coventina was forgotten. She sat at her favourite altar, staring longingly at her precious gifts, remembering the good times. Her nymphs tried to cheer her up but sorrowful tears trickled down her cheeks.

New people moved onto the land. They used the stone from the old fort to construct their farms and houses.

Centuries later another army passed by Coventina's abandoned well. The soldiers built a new road so that they could march quickly from Newcastle to Carlisle.

The heart-broken goddess remained unnoticed and unloved.

Another hundred years passed. Mr Clayton from Chesters, a grand house not far from the well, decided to improve his land by getting rid of the bog. He ordered his men to start digging out drains.

To their amazement they uncovered Coventina's altars, incense burners and gifts.

HOORAY!

They've found my well and all my gifts!

Mr Clayton hurried to call in the archaeologists; they were delighted. They carefully dug out the shrine and Coventina's precious gifts.

DEAE
COVVENTINAE
FDCOSCONIA
NVSPR COH&
I BAT PSLM

Coventina's well was famous. Even the newspapers in London printed the story of its discovery. So many people came to see it that a policeman was put on guard!

Coventina is happy again because people have started to visit her. Some bring her flowers, others coins. What would you bring?

Amy

Connor

Paul

Leigh

Molly

Chloe

Emily

Kerry

Jamie

Morgin

Ceatti

Chantelle

Written and illustrated by
the children of
St Michael's Church of England First School
Alnwick

Tony

Caitlin

Varran

Caitlin

Brett

Rebecca

About the Project

The stories in this book come from Roman myths and legends
as well as the lives of real people who lived in Roman times.
Some of them, like *Hercules the Champion*, are based on
stories hundreds of years old, others, such as *Coventina
the Forgotten Goddess*, are imaginary.

To research their stories the children from St Michael's
and Stobhillgate First Schools looked at artefacts in the
Museum of Antiquities and studied historical writings.
They visited *Seven Stories, the Centre for Children's Books*
to learn how a book is made, right from the very first
creative spark to the moment it appears on the bookshelf.
The next stage was for them to work with their teachers
and our Project staff to put their ideas down in words and images.

Arlene and I have worked carefully to bring together
the children's ideas, text and drawings to create these stories.
We hope that you enjoy them.

Jo Catling

Hercules the Champion

Like many Roman myths, the stories of Hercules come from those told about the gods by the Ancient Greeks.

Hercules' quest to find the golden apples was one of the twelve tasks given to him by Eurystheus at Juno's request. Juno hated Hercules because he was the son of her husband Jupiter by another woman. She hoped he would die during one of the quests. Unfortunately for Juno, Hercules succeeded in all of them and when he eventually died Jupiter made him immortal.

FACTOIDS

The lovely ladies were known as the Hesperides. Legend had it that they were the daughters of Atlas.

The golden apples grew on a tree given to Juno, by Gaia, goddess of the Earth, when she married Jupiter . It was believed that anyone who ate the apples would stay young and beautiful and live forever.

HOW DO YOU SAY IT?	
Eurystheus	U ris thay us
Nereus	Nair ray us
Anateus	An a tay us
Hercules	Her q lees
Libya	Lib ee ah
Illyria	Ill ir yah

LOOK AT THE MAP

Can you find these places in the Classical World?

Egypt

Libya

Illyria

Atlas Mountains

Romulus and Remus - The Terrible Twins

Like the myths of Hercules, the story of Romulus and Remus and the foundation of Rome links the 'new' Roman civilization with the 'old' Greek culture.

Kings Numitor and Amulius were supposed to be descendants of the Greek hero Aeneas. After the battle of Troy he escaped and eventually ended up on the island now known as Sicily. He travelled from here to Italy, where he settled.

FACTOIDS

Rome was founded in 753 BC.

Faustulus was killed in the fight between Romulus and Remus and their supporters. Some people believe that he is buried under the Forum in Rome.

Vestal Virgins looked after the temple of Vesta, the goddess of the hearth, home and family. Their main duty was to make sure that the sacred flame never went out.

HOW DO YOU SAY IT?	
Numitor	New mit or
Amulius	Am u lee us
Tiberius	Tie beer ree us
Faustulus	Fow stew lus
Aeneas	A nee us

LOOK AT THE MAP

Can you find these places in the Classical World?

Roma

Sicily

Hannibal and his Amazing Elephants

Hannibal's march across the Alps in 218 BC is one of the most famous stories from the early history of Rome. Carthage had a huge empire that it lost in battle against the Romans. Hannibal and his father were determined to rebuild their empire.

After he crossed the Alps Hannibal went on to win three major battles against the Romans. He was finally defeated in 202 BC by the great Roman general, Scipio, at the Battle of Zama. The Carthaginian armies were crushed but Hannibal survived.

For many years Hannibal lived in Carthage but moved to help the kings of Syria and Bythynia (part of modern Turkey) in their battles against the Romans. In 183 BC he committed suicide to avoid being captured by the Romans.

FACTOIDS

Zama is in North Africa not far from Hannibal's home in Carthage.

After the Battle of Zama Scipio added Africanus to his name to remind everyone of his great success in defeating Hannibal.

No other enemy of Rome had so much success in battle as Hannibal.

Male elephants will follow female elephants anywhere!

HOW DO YOU SAY IT?	
Hamilcar	Ham ill car
Audax	Ow dax
Carthaginian	Cartha jin ee an
Pyrenees	Pi ren eez
Bythynia	Bith in ee ya

LOOK AT THE MAP

Can you find these places in the Classical World?

Hispania	Bythynia
Carthage	Syria
The Alps	The Pyrenees

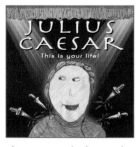

Julius Caesar - This is Your Life!

Julius Caesar is probably the most famous Roman of all. He was a brilliant general as well as a very clever politician. Through his many victories and strong laws he made the Roman Empire very powerful. He organised the calendar that we use today.

However, his success made him many enemies in the Senate. He dismissed them but he didn't take away their wealth and land; this was a mistake as they were still able to plot and fight against him, causing his downfall.

FACTOIDS

Born on July 12th or 13th 100 BC, in Rome. Died in Rome March 15, 44 BC .

Caesar had three wives: Cornelia, Pompeia, daughter of General Pompey, and Calpurnia. Calpurnia dreamt about her husband's death and tried to stop him meeting with the Senate.

Caesar kept diaries about his battles.

Gallia and Gaul are the same place. The Gauls were a Celtic tribe.

'Crossing the Rubicon' is a phrase used to describe a decision from which there is no turning back.

HOW DO YOU SAY IT?	
Vercingetorix	Ver sin get or ix
Cornelia	Cor nee lee ah
Calpurnia	Cal purr nee ah
Pompeia	Pom pay ee ah
aedile	ad ee lay

LOOK AT THE MAP

Can you find these places in the Classical World?

Gallia	Egypt
Italia	Roma
Alesia	River Rubicon
Mediterranean Sea	

Mithras Slays the Bull

The story of Mithras killing the Primeval Bull is a creation myth, an attempt by people who lived many hundreds of years ago to explain how the World and all living plants and creatures were made.

In every temple to Mithras there was a picture of Mithras killing the Bull, similar to the one below. This picture is known as a tauroctony. The sun god and the moon goddess watch as Mithras kills the Bull. His friends Cautes and Cautopates stand beside him.

There is a temple to Mithras near the fort at Carrawburgh along Hadrian's Wall.

Replica of the tauroctony from
Carrawburgh at the Museum of Antiquities

The temple of Mithras at Carrawburgh

FACTOIDS

Mithras was known as the Lord of Light.

He was first worshipped in Persia.

Roman soldiers and traders liked Mithras because he represented strength and truth.

HOW DO YOU SAY IT?

Cautes	Cow tays
Cautopates	Cowt o part ays
Tauroctony	Tor oc tony

Maia's Story

The successful Roman invasion of Britain was led by Emperor Claudius in AD 43. He came at the invitation of Prince Verica of the Atrebates, a tribe that had been trading with the Romans for many years.

It is true that the Emperor brought fifteen war elephants with him but they were only used to frighten the British. They would have had a trainer and, who knows, he may have had a brave daughter like Maia.

When he left Britain Claudius ordered an enormous stone arch to be built at Camulodunum (Colchester) in honour of his conquest of the British people. It was burnt down twenty years later by Boudicca and her warriors.

FACTOIDS

Emperor Claudius stayed in Britain for only sixteen days after the invasion.

It took Claudius about six weeks to travel from Rome to Britain.

There was a great lighthouse at Boulogne.

Elephants really are frightened of pigs!

HOW DO YOU SAY IT?

Aulus Plautius	Owl us Ploor tee us
Togodumnus	Tog oh dum nus
Catuvellauni	Cat ooh vell or nee
Camulodunum	Cam u low do num
Atrebates	At reb ate eez
Boudicca	Boo dik a

LOOK AT THE MAP

Can you find these places in the Classical World?

Massilia

Bononia

Ostia

Roma

Caratacus and Cartimandua - The Britons Fight Back

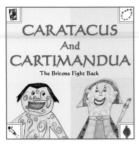

Caratacus was one of the three sons of Cunobelinus. The others were Adminius, and Togodumnus. Adminius was a Roman ally and seen as a traitor by his family. After the invasion Caratacus became a figurehead for all the British leaders as they struggled against Roman rule. In Wales he is known as Caradog.

Unlike a Roman Empress, Cartimandua was queen in her own right. It seems that women in Britain had more rights than Roman women. Archaeologists have found artefacts at Stanwick in Yorkshire that might have come from Cartimandua's capital. We don't know what happened to Cartimandua and Vellocatus. Tacitus, the Roman writer, lost interest in the story once Venutius was defeated.

FACTOIDS

The Romans spoke Latin.

Druids were spiritual leaders of the Celtic tribes.

Unlike most Celts, the Catuvellauni used coins; some had Cunobelinus' head on them.

Camulodunum (Colchester in Essex) was Caratacus' capital.

Shakespeare wrote a play called *Cymbeline* about Caratacus' father.

HOW DO YOU SAY IT?

Caratacus	Ca ra tak us
Togodumnus	Tog oh dum nus
Catuvellauni	Cat ooh vell or nee
Ostorius	Ost or ree us
Brigantes	Brig ant ays
Cartimandua	Cart ee man do er
Venutius	Ven oo tee us
Vellocatus	Vell oh cat us

LOOK AT THE MAP

This story has a map of its own.
Can you find where the Catuvellauni and Brigantes tribes lived?

Julia Lucilla - A Senator's Daughter at the Edge of the Empire

All the characters in this story were real apart from Amelia. We know about them from the tombstone Julia Lucilla put up for her husband and the altar set up by their freedman, Eutychus.

Julia was used to travelling with her husband, but even so, the fort at Bremenium must have been a bleak and lonely place for her to live. We don't know for certain that Julia met the Empress but it is likely that Rufinus came to Britain on the orders of the Emperor to help him keep order on the northern frontier.

FACTOIDS

Emperor Septimus Severus lived in York from AD 208 until he died in AD 211. He was born in Africa.

Rufinus' tombstone is in Elsdon church, Northumberland.

A commanding officer's family left the fort when he died so that the new officer could move in.

HOW DO YOU SAY IT?	
Rufinus	Roo feen us
Petuaria	Pet u ah ree ah
Eutychus	U ti cous
Eburacum	Eh bur a cum
Bremenium	Bre men ee um
Silvanus	Sill varn us
Habitancum	Hab it an cum

LOOK AT THE MAP

Can you find these places on the map of Northern Britannia?

Petuaria

Eburacum

Habitancum

Bremenium

Coria

Coventina the Forgotten Goddess

Not a lot is known about the goddess Coventina except that she had links with wells and springs. In the past people made offerings to gods and goddesses in the hope that they would help heal them or bring them good luck. Today people still throw coins into wells and pools and make a wish.

The site of Coventina's Well is near the fort at Carrawburgh on Hadrian's Wall. There is not a lot to see now, just a boggy area surrounded by a fence.

The altars, incense burners and other objects found when the archaeologists excavated the well in the nineteenth century are on display at Chesters Roman Fort, a few miles west of Carrawburgh.

FACTOIDS

The fort at Carrawburgh was built between AD 130-133 as part of Hadrian's Wall.

General Wade built the road from Newcastle to Carlisle in the 1730's so that soldiers based in Newcastle could march easily to the other side of the country if there was an attack by the Scots.

Coventina's Well was excavated in 1876. Local people took so many things that policemen had to guard the site.

HOW DO YOU SAY IT?	
Carrawburgh	Ca raw bruh
Cilurnum	Si lur num

LOOK AT THE MAP

Can you find these places on the map of Northern Britannia?

Carrawburgh

Hadrian's Wall

Chesters

Throughout the book we have tried to refer to places by their Latin names.
Here they are along with their English names.

COUNTRIES

English	Latin
Egypt	Aegyptus
France	Gallia
Germany	Germania
Greece	Achaia
Great Britain	Britannia
Iraq	Persia
Italy	Italia
Spain	Hispania
Western Balkans	Illyria

TOWNS

English	Latin
Boulogne	Bononia
Brough on Humber	Petuaria
Carrawburgh	Brocolitia
Chesters	Cilurnum
Colchester	Camulodunum
Corbridge	Coria
Dijon	Alesia
High Rochester	Bremenium
Marseilles	Massilia
Rome	Roma
York	Eburacum
Risingham	Habitancum

RIVERS

English	Latin
River	Fluvium
Rhone	Rhodanus
Severn	Sabrina
Thames	Tamesis
Tiber	Tiberis

With thanks to...

All the children, teachers and teaching assistants of
Year 4 Stobhillgate First School, Morpeth and
Years 3 and 4 St Michael's Church of England First School, Alnwick.

Thank you to
Rebecca and Victoria Adcock,
Tyler Bayliss,
Chelsea and Conrad Bria
and Harry Nordemann
for additional illustrations.

We would also like to thank
Seven Stories, the Centre for Children's Books
The Design Desk
Barbara Hutchinson
Gigi Ming Stones
Sarah Bethell
and
all the staff at the Museum of Antiquities.

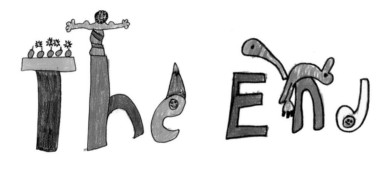